The Wizard of Sound

The Wizard of Sound

A Story about Thomas Edison

by Barbara Mitchell
illustrations by Hetty Mitchell

SCHOLASTIC INC.
New York   Toronto   London   Auckland   Sydney

For Brian

Text copyright © 1991 by Barbara Mitchell.
Illustrations copyright © 1991 by Carolrhoda Books, Inc.
All rights reserved. Published by Scholastic Inc., 555 Broadway, New York, NY 10012, by arrangement with Carolrhoda Books, Inc.
Printed in the U.S.A.
ISBN 0-590-48529-6

1 2 3 4 5 6 7 8 9 10   **23**   01 00 99 98 97 96 95 94

Table of Contents

Boy Scientist   7

Traveling Telegrapher   16

From Telegraph to Telephone   28

The Machine Must Talk   42

The Wizard   50

Afterword   61

Thomas Edison's
    Major Inventions   62

Bibliography   63

① Boy Scientist

Poison. Al placed the carefully labeled bottle on its shelf and reached into the bushel basket beside him for another. The just-washed bottles had been gathered from all over town. They would soon hold the chemicals he used for his experiments. His collection was growing. He had over two hundred bottles now, every one of them marked *poison* so that no one would disturb them.

There were no other children in the big old house to meddle with the bottles and heaps of wire and scrap iron that made up Al's cellar laboratory. Twelve-year-old Thomas Alva was the baby of the family. (His mother called him Alva. Friends called him Al.) Three of Al's brothers and sisters were grown-up. The other three had died before he was a year old. Al had nearly died himself from scarlet fever in 1854 when he was seven. That was the year his family had moved to Port Huron, Michigan, from Milan, Ohio.

Al had caught colds every winter since, and they nearly always settled in his ears. The insides of his ears would swell and fill up with fluid. There were no antibiotics in the 1850s to clear up ear infections, and doctors didn't yet know how to use tubes to remove fluid from children's ears. Nancy Edison doctored her son as best she could with medicines from the drugstore shelves. That was why Al was home from school that day with cotton stuffed in his aching ears.

Al was perfectly happy shut up in his laboratory for the day. Scientific experiments were his love, especially those having to do with electricity. Lately he had been concentrating his efforts on a machine called the telegraph, invented by Samuel F. B. Morse.

Morse's invention was the talk of the times. News had spread slowly in the early 1800s, before the telegraph. The telephone had not yet been invented. Businesses had depended on messengers to get information to other people in the same city. To send mail to other cities, people had depended on the stagecoach and the pony express.

Families had had to wait for months to hear from distant relatives. Morse had found a way to spread news almost instantly. His telegraph sent messages over a wire by alternately making and breaking an electrical connection. This caused an iron bar at the message's destination to hit a magnet, making a tapping sound. Morse had worked out a code with long and short taps. Different combinations of taps represented different letters of the alphabet.

The first telegraph message had been sent in 1844—from Washington, D.C., to Boston—three years before Al was born. By the 1850s, telegraph lines stretched from Boston to Chicago. The magical messages would soon reach clear to California, it was said.

Al had built a working Morse telegraph of his own. It was made up of a transmitter, which sent messages, and a receiver, which received them. He and his friend Dick had strung a telegraph line between their neighboring houses. Then they had persuaded the teacher who boarded with the Edisons to teach them Morse code. The two boys idolized the young telegraphers who followed the fast-developing telegraph system from city to city, tapping out messages.

One night at supper, Sam and Nancy Edison

had a message of their own for their son. They had had a talk with his teacher. Thomas Alva would never make a student, the teacher had said. Keeping him in school was a waste of time. The news came as a relief to Al. School had been an unhappy experience from the very beginning.

Al remembered being placed in the school of the Reverend and Mrs. G. B. Engle soon after his recovery from scarlet fever when he was seven. He'd been there for only three months when he heard the Reverend Engle say to his wife that the Edison boy's brain seemed to be "addled." Al had run home and reported the hurtful information to his mother. She knew an intelligent child when she saw one, former teacher Nancy Edison had declared hotly. She'd withdrawn her son from the school, bought him a science book that she knew would capture his heart, and proceeded to teach him herself.

Keeping Al away from a classroom full of children was no good, Sam Edison had told his wife. Why, the boy did not even bother with boys in the neighborhood. So Al had been placed in a second school, taught by Mr. P. L. Hubbard. Al was happier there. The discipline was less strict. But the teacher complained that Al did not pay attention. Al said the teacher spoke too softly. He missed so many days due to illness that he was always behind in his work.

Nancy coddled the boy, his father had said when Al was withdrawn from the second school. Sam Edison worried about his youngest son. Al was sickly looking and very small, except for what many folks considered to be an unusually large head. Was the large head on his son's frail shoulders a sign that there really was a problem with the boy's brain? When Al turned eleven, he'd been sent to Port Huron's new public school. Perhaps the first public school in town would be the answer, his parents had hoped.

Now it was the same thing all over again. Al was no good at sports. The other students called him names and did not want him on their teams. The teacher said Thomas Alva asked questions when he should have been giving answers. When he did offer an answer, it usually had little to do with the teacher's question. And yet Al was a good reader. He finished assignments long before the others in the class. To relieve his boredom, he kicked the boy in front of him. There was no doubt about it. Thomas Alva was a problem.

And so it was decided. Al would leave school

for good and go to work. It was not unusual for a boy to leave school in his early teens in those days. Nancy was not worried about Al's education. Her son had developed a real hunger for reading, and she knew he would continue to study on his own. Al's father got him a job selling newspapers and refreshments on the new Grand Trunk Railroad, which ran between Port Huron and Detroit.

The sixty-three-mile run to Detroit took four hours. There was a five-hour wait before the return to Port Huron. Al took advantage of the five hours of free time by working in the miniature laboratory he had installed in the baggage car. All went well until a sudden lurch of the train ignited some chemicals and set the wooden car on fire. The conductor requested that the laboratory be removed. So Al joined the Detroit Public Library and spent his free hours reading science books instead.

It was while serving his customers that Al first noticed a real problem with his hearing. When the train was moving and the passengers had to raise their voices above the roar of the engine, he could hear their requests. When the train stopped and the passengers spoke in normal voices, he could not make out what they were saying to him.

Al's parents took him to the doctor. The hearing problem had likely begun back when their son had been stricken with scarlet fever, the doctor told them. The many ear infections that had followed had permanently damaged his middle ear. There was nothing that could be done for him.

By the time Al had worked the train job for three years, his father was becoming concerned. There was not much future in selling candy and newspapers. In February Al would turn sixteen, and it was time he learned a trade. But what? Al hated farm work. He showed no interest in carpentry and sales, his father's lines of work. What was to become of him?

Al knew exactly what he wanted to do. He wanted to be a telegrapher. A neighbor's cow had knocked down the poles that supported Al's new mile-and-a-half-long telegraph lines. Al had had enough of amateur telegraphy. He was ready to turn professional. James MacKenzie, telegrapher at the Mount Clemens railroad station and a friend of the family, was training an apprentice. He offered to take Al on as well. Mount Clemens was halfway between Port Huron and Detroit. Al figured he could get another boy to work the second lap of his train run and study with MacKenzie for part of each day.

Sam Edison had doubts about the idea. He still wondered about Al's intelligence. And then there was the hearing problem. Fooling around with wires strung across the meadow was one thing. Sending and receiving messages that reported the location of fast-moving trains would be quite another. Could a boy with a hearing problem be trusted to do the job? But Al's mother knew that her son could do anything he set his mind to.

Al insisted he could hear the tap-tap of the telegraph with no problem at all. In fact, he said, not being able to hear distracting sounds around him would only help him in his new career.

② Traveling Telegrapher

Al and his mother had their way. Al showed up at the Mount Clemens telegraph office eager to learn. In fact he was so eager that he brought along his own telegraph instruments, which he had made himself. But he would not be needing them. James MacKenzie used a set of original Morse instruments to help his students learn. Morse's telegraph receiver had a device that penciled messages in Morse code onto a strip of paper. The long and short taps were recorded as dashes and dots. These marks could then be "decoded" into letters. Eventually telegraphers learned to recognize the letters by sound as they were tapped out by the telegraph. After that there was no longer a need for the paper strips, so new telegraphs didn't have them. The outdated method had a definite advantage for Al, though. What he could not get by ear, he could read from the strip.

Mrs. MacKenzie had her own teaching method.

Each time her husband's young students increased their speed on the telegraph, she would reward them with a fresh-baked apple pie. Within five months, Al had learned all MacKenzie had to teach him. And he had developed quite a liking for apple pie. A telegraph office had opened in a corner of Thomas Walker's jewelry store in Port Huron. When the store's telegrapher left to join the Civil War, Al took over the part-time job.

The Port Huron telegraph office was not at all busy. Al was soon spending much of his time mixing chemicals and toying with electricity. It was not unusual for Mr. Walker to have his peaceful work interrupted by a startling BOOM. Discovering that his fine watchmaker's tools, which Al had borrowed, had been dulled cutting wire and damaged by acid did little to calm the jeweler's jangled nerves. Perhaps the young telegrapher was ready to move on to a busier office, Walker suggested.

The idea of joining the traveling telegraphers he had admired as a boy appealed to Al. Roving about the country spelled adventure. It also meant the opportunity to increase his skill as a telegrapher. When MacKenzie recommended him for the Stratford, Ontario, office, Al gladly accepted the job. No more selling candy and sandwiches for him. He was not yet seventeen years old, but he was a real telegrapher.

Al would spend the next four years working in one dingy telegraph office after another. From Canada he went to Michigan and then to Ohio. The gypsylike life did not bother him. Al had never cared about fancy clothes or living places. He spent his pay on his experiments and lived in inexpensive boardinghouses. The conditions often tested his ingenuity, which was just what Al enjoyed. At one place, he invented an electrical device for zapping cockroaches.

What did bother Al was the loneliness he felt. The other telegraphers did not take to the new operator from Port Huron. Al was not interested in going out with them after work. He never dated a girl. He did not join in on conversations. Al never let on, but the truth was that his poor hearing made it hard for him to follow a discussion. He did not want a fuss made over his handicap, so he simply stood shyly aside. The impression was that this "oddball" wanted to be left alone.

Deep down, Al wanted very badly to fit in. Perhaps if he were amusing, the other fellows might accept him, he reasoned. He resorted to one of his favorite entertainments, playing practical jokes. Outside one telegraph office, there was a pump with a metal drinking cup hanging beside it. Al had a sudden inspiration—he would electrify the cup. But the telegraphers who received a shock when they went for a cool drink of water were even less likely to strike up a friendship with Al.

When an opening came up at the busy Indianapolis telegraph office in 1864, Al got the job. Al was a "novice," or beginning, operator. He could take down messages at about fifteen words per minute. He wanted to advance to an "expert" speed of more than thirty words per minute. Every night after work, he and another novice would sit beside the expert telegrapher as he worked. The telegrapher received the news from the equally expert sender on the other end of the wire at a fast forty-five words per minute. Al hoped to increase his own receiving speed by watching the expert operator. But with his poor hearing, he was unable to decode the rapid sounds.

To Al's mind, no problem was unsolvable. In a corner of the office, he found some old Morse instruments like those he had used at MacKenzie's. Al discovered a way to slow down the speed of the message by hooking two of the machines together. He and the other novice practiced every night, increasing their speeds little by little. But the makeshift arrangement tended to break down and cause the entire newsroom to fall behind.

The hookup he had invented gave Al an idea. There was a limit to the distance a telegraph message could travel on a wire before static interfered. After two hundred miles, the messages had to be retransmitted. Why couldn't an old-style Morse telegraph be hooked up to a transmitter to repeat messages automatically? he asked himself. Al began to spend much of his time experimenting with what he called his telegraph repeater. Much to his delight, the idea worked. His boss, however, was not so pleased. Edison spent far too much time fiddling. Al's constant meddling with the equipment made the first-class telegraphers angry. Al was very unpopular. Within five months, he had moved on to Cincinnati, Ohio.

Wherever he went, Al's personality and constant experimenting caused him problems. From Ohio he moved on to Tennessee. From there he went to Louisville, Kentucky. In Louisville Al had a frightening experience. He had discovered a stack of scientific magazines at an auction and was lugging them home after work at three in the morning. "Stop!" a voice rang out. Al walked on. Suddenly a bullet whizzed by him. Al turned and came face to face with a policeman. The officer had thought Al was a thief. Al explained that he had not heard the command. The near brush with death brought home an unhappy truth. Al's hearing was growing worse.

Al also made a happy discovery in Louisville. He found that what he really liked about telegraphy was the machinery itself—experimenting with it, thinking of ways to improve it. He had an idea for a duplex, or double, telegraph that would improve telegraphy one hundred percent. The duplex telegraph would send two messages at the same time. Other telegraphers were experimenting with the idea, too, but Al wanted to be the first to build a workable model. Al's boss thought it couldn't be done. Any fool knew that a wire could not be worked in both directions at once, he said.

Al was as determined as ever. He kept the office in constant turmoil with his experiments. When a container of sulfuric acid slipped out of his hand and dripped through the flooring onto expensive new furniture in the room below, he was fired. Late in the fall of 1867, Al went home.

He was practically penniless. Although he had not yet developed a working duplex, every cent he could save had gone into his experiments.

He no longer wished to be a telegrapher, Al informed his parents. What he really wanted to be was an inventor. It was a darn fool idea, Sam Edison said. Inventors starved. For the first time in her life, Nancy feared that her son would end up a failure. Nancy was not well. While Al had been gone, his thirty-one-year-old sister, Harriet Ann, had died. The loss of yet another of her children had been too much for Nancy. Al was shocked to find his strong, supportive mother nervous and in a state of mental confusion.

When a friend told him about an opening for a telegrapher in Boston's Western Union office, Al managed to get a free pass from the railroad and went to claim the job. Being a telegrapher no longer enchanted him, it was true. But inventing would take money. Al also had another reason for going to Boston. The city was known as the center of electrical invention.

Al arrived at the very proper Western Union office in his usual style. He had on a pair of jeans that were too short, a rumpled flannel shirt that was frayed at the cuffs, and a hat with a torn brim.

His shaggy brown hair stood up every which way, as always. The dignified Boston supervisor took one look at the countrified new telegrapher and assigned him to the number-one wire to receive copy for the *Boston Herald*. The fastest sender in New York was on the other end. The assignment was meant to be a joke, but Al, who had never lacked confidence when it came to his work, did a fine job.

Al's poor coordination prevented him from ever becoming a good sender. But he had developed into a lightning-quick receiver. To compensate for his poor hearing, he had made use of a couple of tricks. Most receivers worked so fast that they had no idea what the messages they took actually said. Al made himself concentrate on content. Telegraphers wrote in a hasty scrawl in order to keep up their speed. The printers who received their work were used to handling half-finished words. When a message came faster than Al's damaged ears could handle it, he either filled in words he thought fit the meaning or simply made a scribble and trusted the printer to fill it in.

Once he was settled in his new job, Al lost no time in seeking out a Boston man he had heard of named Charles Williams. Williams manufactured telegraphic and electrical equipment and was known to encourage all types of invention. Inventors were always welcome to sit down with him for a chat. The talk usually led to the offer of space for their experimenting and equipment at a discount price. Al was soon filling page after page with inventive ideas.

The pages of "crazy-looking" drawings did little to increase Al's popularity at Western Union. His fellow telegraphers began referring to their dreamy-eyed colleague as "the loony." Al spent more and more time at Williams's shop. There he felt at home. At work he took to playing practical jokes again, and he experimented into the wee hours of the night on Western Union's equipment. His employer soon let it be known that Al's resignation would be welcome.

Al was only too happy to oblige. In January of 1869, he placed an announcement in a trade magazine. Thomas A. Edison could hereafter be found at the shop of Charles Williams on Court Street, where he would devote his time to bringing out inventions, it read.

3

From Telegraph to Telephone

Where does a hungry inventor with no money find something to eat in New York City? Al asked himself. He wandered down to the docks along the river.

The move to Charles Williams's shop in Boston had led to disappointment. Al's first task had been to convince a Boston businessman to loan him five hundred dollars toward his work on the duplex telegraph. Al had used up almost all of the money trying to perfect his invention. Frank L. Pope, one of the most respected telegraphers in the United States, had offered to let Al test his duplex on the telegraph line between Rochester and New York City. So, Al had left with great excitement for Rochester, New York, on the last of the borrowed money. Sadly, the duplex had let him down. The machine that had worked like a dream in Williams's little shop failed when put to the test on the long, exposed wires between Rochester and New York.

Now here he was, jobless and penniless again, with the news ringing in his ears that another inventor was about to present a perfected duplex. At last a dockhand gave Al a sample packet of imported teas, but tea wouldn't satisfy his hunger. Al continued his walk. In the chill of the morning, a familiar aroma filled the air—the delicious smell of apples baking. Warm memories of Mrs. MacKenzie's apple pies flooded Al's mind. He followed his nose. Yes, the man at the counter said, he would be willing to swap a packet of fine imported teas for coffee and a hot apple dumpling. Apple dumplings were Thomas Edison's favorite food for the rest of his life.

Al had no money to pay for a place to stay,

but Frank Pope came to his aid again. He had arranged for Al to sleep on a cot at Laws Reporting Telegraph, where Pope was the superintendent. One day, not long after Al had moved into the office, the company's entire gold indicator system broke down. The system was made up of machines that printed out the constantly changing prices of gold. "Fix it, fix it!" the worried Mr. Laws cried. It was Al who discovered a loose spring and repaired the system.

He knew of a way to guarantee that the system would never again break down all at once, Al said. And furthermore, he was at work on an improved version of Laws's invention, called a stock ticker. Al was hired as an assistant. A job! To Al's way of thinking, that meant money for inventing.

Happily living on apple dumplings and coffee, Al poured his salary into his experiments. He never did worry about proper nutrition. He didn't bother himself about getting eight hours of sleep each night, either. Al had developed the habit of taking little naps whenever and wherever he could fit them in. His fellow workers grew used to the sight of their inventor friend curled up as cozy as a cat on a workbench.

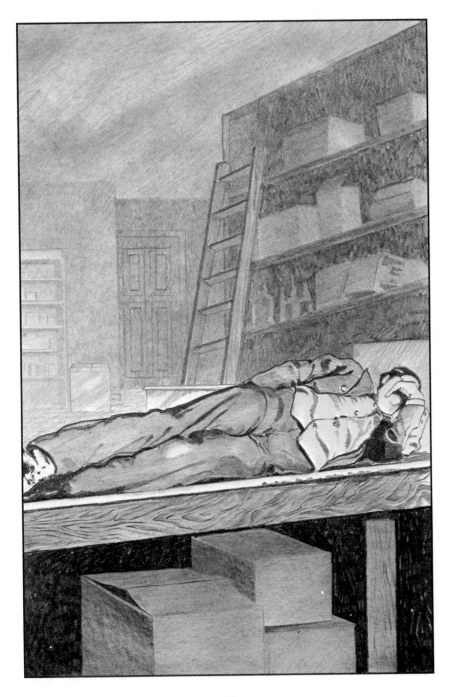

When Laws sold out to the Gold & Stock Telegraph Company, Gold & Stock invested in Al's stock ticker. Al rushed to the bank with a check for fifteen hundred dollars. He had never before received so much money at once. Al's hearing tended to be even worse when he was excited or upset. The teller mumbled something that he did not hear. Embarrassed, Al rushed out of the building, back to Gold & Stock. The bank would not give him his money, he reported. It turned out that the teller had been reminding him that he had forgotten to sign the check.

Al continued to improve the stock ticker. When Gold & Stock merged with Western Union, Western Union offered thirty thousand dollars for Al's newest version of the stock ticker, called a gold printer. Twenty-three-year-old Al was overjoyed. He could hardly believe that Western Union, the leading supporter of invention in the United States, had bought his first big invention. Within a week, he had spent the entire thirty thousand dollars.

The money had gone to set up a shop in Newark, New Jersey, to manufacture his gold printers. Al was going into business for himself. He bought the finest equipment. He hired the finest workers.

Two of those men would become very important to his career as an inventor. Al had no talent for drawing. To turn his rough sketches into expertly drawn plans, he hired draftsman Charles Batchelor. To turn Batchelor's drawings into working models, he hired machinist John Kruesi.

The joy of setting up his own business was dampened by a telegram. Al's mother, his strongest supporter, had died. "If it had not been for her faith in me, I very likely would not have been an inventor," he said. Shattered by the loss, he threw himself into his work. He often worked eighteen hours a day, supervising, making business contacts, handling finances—and, of course, inventing.

One of the workers hired to punch holes in telegraphic tape was a sixteen-year-old girl named Mary Stilwell. Al found Mary attractive. But every time he thought of speaking to her, he was overcome by his old shyness. At last the solution came to him. He would use his deafness as an excuse to stand close to Mary. Like most of Al's experiments, this one was a success. He and Mary were married on Christmas Day 1871.

The new bride did not see much of her husband. Al was becoming more and more fascinated with working with sound. He spent hours pouring over studies by European scientists on sound production. At the same time, he was working on a high-speed telegraph. He was also developing his duplex into a quadruplex, a telegraph that could send two messages in each direction at the same time. When he could fit it in, he was researching the harmonic telegraph. Elisha Gray, a Chicago electrician, already had two patents on this telegraph, which could send musical tones over a wire.

Somehow Al found time to run his business. The pace was exhausting, even for ambitious Thomas Alva Edison. And despite all his hard work, Al was deeply in debt. Money management was not one of his talents. Al had a most unusual way of handling bills. He simply hung them on a hook until the sender pestered him further. Mary had no more talent for managing money than her young husband. Knowing that his bride was often lonesome due to his long workdays, Al allowed her to buy anything she desired. Mary bought fancy gowns and hats. She paid high prices for fancy foods. She never stopped to add up the cost. The high rent Al paid on their Newark house did not help.

In 1875 Al made a decision. He would no longer involve himself in manufacturing. Instead he would start a new business devoted entirely to invention. He found an inexpensive house set on a large piece of land in Menlo Park, New Jersey, about twenty-five miles south of New York City. Mary signed for the mortgage. (Al's credit was not acceptable.) Al sent for his carpenter father to oversee the construction of a large barnlike building on his new property. The shop would be painted a fresh country white, and it would be surrounded by a sturdy picket fence. Al wasn't taking any chances on roving cows ruining his experiments this time.

From the outside, the white shop surrounded by apple trees and blackberry bushes did not look much different from other structures in the little farm community. The inside, however, was something else. The long, two-story laboratory, which was quite elaborate for its time, held shelf after shelf of the finest scientific materials available. There were boxes and jars of every chemical imaginable, batteries, a gaslight apparatus, a steam engine, and a well-equipped photographic darkroom. A small building in front of the laboratory contained Al's office and a library. To the rear of the laboratory, there was a machine shop. Al brought seventeen of his very best workers with him from Newark.

Al's workers would no longer have to produce machinery for sale. Their only job would be to experiment with and build models of the inventions their boss dreamed up. The idea was startling. Doctors and professors experimented. No one in the world had ever devoted an entire business to invention.

Al was not the only inventor trying to make the telegraph do tricks. Alexander Graham Bell (another Boston inventor who had worked at the shop of Charles Williams), Elisha Gray, and several others were working on harmonic telegraphs, too. The notes that Gray's harmonic telegraph sent over the wire were made by tuning forks. Al was experimenting with using notes from other musical instruments, among them the dulcimer and the cornet. If music could be sent over the telegraph, the inventors reasoned, then so could the human voice! Everyone wanted to be the first to send the sound of a person speaking over wire. Western Union offered to pay Al five hundred dollars a month to make them the winner.

The race was on. Al's work did not go easily.

The only way he could hear sound coming over his experimental instruments was to bite into them. This allowed the sound vibrations to be conducted through the bones of his head—past his damaged middle ear—to the inner hearing nerve. Al also suffered from painful earaches. Mary's sister Alice, who had moved in with the Edisons to keep Mary company, once came upon Al grinding his feet into the carpet because the pain in his ears was so intense. The doctor Al consulted said that he had developed arthritis of the bones of the ear. But despite the pain, Al kept working.

Western Union wasn't happy with Al's work. "Our desks are littered with Edison's unsuccessful traps," they complained. The slow progress on the speaking telegraph and pressure from Western Union were frustrating.

It was a difficult time for Mary, as well. Her husband found moments of relaxation swapping stories with the Menlo Park farmers. His hearty laugh was a familiar sound at the combined post office-general store. Seated in their cozy circle, hand cupped to his better ear, Al took in the talk. There was little visiting among the farmers' wives, however, and their infrequent socializing did not include Mary Edison. Lace curtains at the windows, plush oriental carpets, and the snappy carriage sweeping down their rutted roads did not sit well with them. It was common knowledge that Mrs. Edison employed three servants to do her housework. This was something that the hardworking farmers' wives would not even dream of. The country women considered citified Mary "uppity."

On Valentine's Day, Alexander Graham Bell filed for a patent on a completed speaking telegraph, or telephone, as he called it. Elisha Gray filed just hours behind him. The race had been close. Al had lost. Bell's telephone created a sensation at the 1876 Centennial celebration in Philadelphia that summer. For all practical purposes, though, the invention left a lot to be desired. Its messages could not travel for more than two miles. The speaker had to shout each sentence three or four times to be heard. As Al said, words with *S*'s in them sounded like a basket of hissing snakes.

"Make us a telephone that works," Western Union begged. Al was happy to oblige. He worked on the telephone all through the fall and winter. At last he thought he had discovered the problem.

Bell's combined transmitter-receiver was not powerful enough to do both jobs. So Al put together a separate transmitter. The new transmitter helped, but the telephone still needed some work.

Then Al had another idea. Bell's telephone, like the telegraph, required only a "make-and-break" current, which is an electrical current that starts and stops. For a more successful telephone, the current would have to be steady. What Al needed to come up with was the material that would conduct, or transmit, this strong, continuous current.

Al put his workers on round-the-clock shifts. Often he slept on a blanket in the corner of the lab, not going home for days. He and his men tested every chemical on the shelves, trying to come up with one that would make Bell's telephone louder, clearer, and able to carry messages over longer distances. He found the answer at last in a simple button of carbon. "Telephone perfected this morning at five A.M. Got a quarter column newspaper every word," he happily reported in his notebook entry for July 17, 1877. The Bell-Edison telephone would be used for the next fifty years.

The many months spent on the telephone had led to a startling surprise for Al. He was on the verge of an invention that would outdo even the work of the sensational Professor Bell. His work with the Bell telephone had turned up a discovery that, as Al himself said, was "downright spooky."

The Machine Must Talk

Al adjusted a gear on the mechanical toy that sat on his workbench, and he glanced at the clock. He had finished just in time. Dot would be coming with his lunch. The Edisons had two children now, five-year-old Marion and year-old Thomas Alva Edison, Jr. Al had nicknamed them Dot and Dash after the Morse code.

Shout into the funnel, Dot was told when she arrived. Dot did as her father instructed. The little paper man connected to the funnel began sawing wood. The sound of Dot's voice had actually made his arm move! Al was every bit as tickled as his daughter. He had made the toy to prove a theory that had grown out of his telephone experiments. Al had noticed that sound would make the flexible disk, or diaphragm, on Bell's telephone receiver vibrate. He had an idea that these vibrations could be put to work, and Dot's toy proved he was right.

Could she take her new toy to the beach that weekend? Dot wanted to know. It was June, the beginning of the season at the shore. Al looked forward to these Sunday outings, although it was not often that he was able to get away. Even at the beach, Al's thoughts were likely to turn to inventing. And these days, that meant he thought about the telephone.

Despite all the excitement over the telephone, nobody was sure just how useful it would be. In 1877 the idea of putting telephones in homes or using them for conversation had not yet been seriously considered. The telephone would be useful in business, its inventors had implied. But businesses were not convinced. They saw this new invention as an inefficient replacement for the telegraph. It was necessary to speak slowly over the telephone to be understood. And people in business figured they would have to pay someone to take down the messages that came over the telephone. Why slow down business when the lightning-quick telegraph could do the job so much more easily? they asked.

But Al had another idea. There was no need to hire people to take messages, Al said. The job could be done by machine—his machine.

European scientists had shown that each sound had its own shape. Al believed he could put these shapes down on paper with his latest invention, the embossing telegraph repeater. The embosser he was experimenting with pressed the shapes of sounds onto waxed paper disks. The sound-shapes could afterward be translated into alphabet letters.

Working with the disk was awkward, so Al substituted a roll of wax-coated paper for the disk. To keep the paper moving evenly, he added a steel spring. Just as Al had expected, the mechanism pressed the sound-shapes onto the waxed paper. Al had known that the sounds would make indentations, but what he didn't know was that the indentations would make sounds! When the end of the spring struck the indentations in the paper, the spring gave off a faint, rhythmic humming sound.

The noises coming from the embossing telegraph repeater sounded amazingly like those Al had heard on the first Bell telephone. Suppose these were human sounds coming from that machine! Now *here* was something to experiment with.

Al placed a roll of wax-coated paper under a

diaphragm with a blunt pin attached to the diaphragm's center. Then he pulled the strip of paper past the pin while shouting, "HALLOO!" The vibration of the diaphragm scratched indentations into the paper. Al pulled the paper through again so that the indentations struck a pin in a second diaphragm, making the diaphragm vibrate. He and Charles Batchelor listened breathlessly.

Faintly, but distinctly, the machine whispered, "Halloo . . ." Al no longer thought about telegraph repeaters, which only recorded sound. Now his mind turned to creating a telephone repeater, a machine that could record and play back sound. By the end of the summer, Al was calling his invention in progress a phonograph.

The painstaking experimentation went on for four months. On November 29, Al made a rough sketch of his phonograph in the daily notebook he kept. On the night of December 3, draftsmen Charles Batchelor and Jim Adams refined the drawing. The next morning, they gave the drawing to machinist John Kruesi. What was the new little machine he was to build supposed to do? Kruesi asked. "The machine must talk," Al said quietly.

Kruesi thought the whole idea was absurd.

Nevertheless, at the end of thirty hours' work, he presented his boss with a neat little machine of brass and iron, with a speaker, for speaking into, mounted on one side and a reproducer on the other. The instrument would use a needle to cut grooves into a tinfoil-covered cylinder as a crank was turned, just as Al had asked.

Everyone in the lab gathered around as Al fitted a piece of tinfoil onto the grooved cylinder. Kruesi expressed the opinion that the machine would not work. Al bet Kruesi two dollars that the machine would indeed talk. And the rest of the workers would owe him a box of cigars, he said.

Al turned the handle of the cylinder and, placing his lips against the speaker, bellowed,

> Mary had a little lamb.
> Its fleece was white as snow.
> And everywhere that Mary went,
> the lamb was sure to go.

The onlookers exchanged amused smiles.

Al disengaged the speaker, moved the reproducer against the cylinder, and turned the crank again. He heard nothing. "I guess you've won the cigars," he said sadly.

Kruesi's mouth hung open. "God in heaven," he muttered in German. A high-pitched, nasal voice—too soft for Al to hear—was coming from the machine. There could be no doubt that it was the voice of Thomas Edison.

The excited workers spent all night with their boss, talking and singing into the machine, and making adjustments. On the morning of December 6, 1877, Al proclaimed his speaking phonograph a success. Thomas Alva Edison, the young man who could barely hear, had invented a machine that could talk.

⑤

The Wizard

The room was overflowing with people. At the back, a janitor worked away at removing the doors from their hinges to make room for the crowd that had surged into the Washington, D.C., meeting hall. The occasion was the spring 1878 meeting of the National Academy of Sciences. The guest of honor was a shy-looking man who appeared to have just gotten out of bed. His hair stood up every which way, and he was doing his best to ignore the commotion around him. An expectant hush settled over the audience.

Out of the silence came the tinny voice of a machine: "The Speaking Phonograph has the honor of presenting itself to the Academy of Sciences." The guest of honor, Thomas Edison, nodded to Charles Batchelor. Batchelor spoke into the machine. When the phonograph repeated his words, a young lady in the audience fainted.

Batchelor crowed like a rooster. The rooster crowed back. Down went another young lady.

That night the president of the United States made a special request. He and the first lady wished to hear the machine that could talk. President and Mrs. Hayes sat up listening to the marvelous machine until three-thirty in the morning. When Edison and Batchelor were requested to perform before Congress, one senator insisted on working the phonograph in a room by himself. His suspicion that the inventor was a ventriloquist was soon replaced by amazement.

Everywhere the phonograph went, it caused a sensation. Like Bell's first telephone, the infant phonograph had a long way to go before it would be practical. Tinfoil "records" did not last long. The sound was scratchy. Turning a crank was not the best way to make a recording. Al, with his usual confidence, did not wait for these imperfections to be worked out. He immediately hired a publicity man to arrange for the phonograph to be exhibited at country fairs. Charles Batchelor designed a beautiful parlor model of the phonograph. Before long "phonograph parlors," like the movie parlors that would follow, had sprung up all over the country. Enchanted listeners paid their pennies to hear for themselves the machine that could talk.

Suddenly Al was no longer just plain Al Edison. A person who could make a machine talk could invent anything, people believed. Now Al was referred to as Professor Thomas Edison, America's number-one inventor. Some went so far as to accuse him of being a wizard. The new Thomas Edison did not mind these titles at all. They certainly beat being called the loony, he said.

So many curious visitors flocked to see "the wizard of Menlo Park" that the railroad had to put extra cars on the line. Surrounded by his enthralled audiences, Professor Edison would pat his machine and ask, "How are you getting on down there?" Then he would crank up the phonograph and it would talk back to him. Much to his surprise, Al found that he actually enjoyed putting on the little performances and showing his guests around the laboratory. The old shyness was gone at last.

On the other hand, being a "wizard" was wearing. Al had returned from Washington ill from overwork. The long, tense hours he had spent working with sound had caught up with him. What he needed was a vacation. When

Professor George F. Barker invited him to join a group of scientists going out West to observe a solar eclipse, Al gratefully accepted. Mary, who was expecting their third child, was not feeling well enough to make the trip to the Rocky Mountains.

One night in the mountains, Al was awakened out of a sound sleep by a loud banging at his cabin door. It was Texas Jack, the fastest gunslinger in the West. To Al's dismay, the man said he was looking for Thomas Edison. When Al identified himself, Texas Jack merely stared at him. He had simply wanted to meet the fellar who had invented the phonograph, he said. He pulled out his gun, fired out the window, and went on his way. The experience far surpassed the eclipse, Al said.

The other scientists on the expedition were interested in experimenting with light. They wanted to know if Al would take part in some work using electricity to produce light. Here was a new avenue of invention! It was just what Al's tired body and spirit needed. He decided to put aside all serious work on the phonograph, his pet invention, to work on the electric light and the electrical power station.

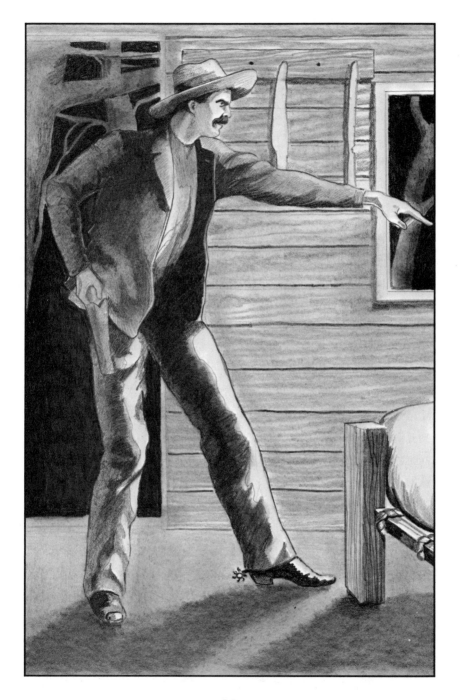

It was fortunate that Al had his work to sustain him. He was about to enter one of the saddest periods of his life. Mary never completely recovered from the birth of Will, their third child, in 1878. She suffered from painful headaches. Her nervousness and anxiety had increased to the point that she could not be left alone. Al was deeply concerned. By the fall of 1883, Mary was no longer able to care for herself and the big house at Menlo Park. Al left his work with the New York Power Station to take her to Florida that winter for a two-month rest.

When they returned in the spring, Mary learned that her father was deathly ill. The news was too much for her. Mary became irrational, and Al had to hire a full-time nurse. The children did not make their usual trips to the shore that summer because their mother was too ill to leave home. Al awakened Dot early in the morning on August 9, 1884. He was barely able to speak. Mary had died in the night.

Gentle Mary was only twenty-nine years old when she died. She had never been accepted by her neighbors. She had spent her life alone in the old country house while her husband was wrapped up in his work. Just how unhappy had his wife been? Al wondered. And how much had unhappiness contributed to her illness? Al was haunted not only by the loss, but also by the cause of his wife's early death. Both his mother and his wife had died of a disease that had affected their minds, and this frightened Al. Mary's death certificate said she died of "congestion of the brain." Doctors now believe she suffered from a brain tumor.

Unable to bear the sight of Menlo Park, Al closed up the house and moved into New York City. The famous laboratory, home of the phonograph and over one hundred forty other inventions, fell to ruin.

Al was still recovering from Mary's death when concerned friends introduced him to a young woman named Mina Miller. Mina was just what Al needed. They were married in February of 1886. Mina Miller was different from any woman Al had ever met. When he stared at her, she stared right back. Being married to a wizard was not easy, Mina admitted to a reporter. But if any woman could "manage" the famous inventor, it was she. Mina insisted that her husband eat. She insisted that he take time off to be with his children. But she also understood her husband's burning desire to invent. Al adored Mina, and he bought her Glenmont, a mansion in West Orange, New Jersey, to prove it.

By the time he married Mina, Al had been away from the phonograph for ten years. Because of the machine's imperfections, the excitement over the phonograph had died down only a year or so after it had been introduced. It no longer made appearances at phonograph parlors and country fairs. Al didn't worry about other inventors working on his talking machine. He really didn't think it had much commercial value.

For once in his life, Al was wrong about the value of one of his inventions. When he realized that businessmen and inventors had been working on the phonograph during his ten years away from it, he knew it was time to turn his attention back to his pet invention.

In December of 1886, Al caught a bad cold. By January it had turned into pneumonia, and he nearly died. As he lay flat on his back, an exciting dream took shape. He would build a new laboratory. The spectacular new facility next to the Edisons' mansion in New Jersey would be a "factory of creativity." The main activity there would be the improvement of the phonograph.

"The phonograph is my baby," Al declared. He threw himself into work on its improvement. His brainchild did have a few minor flaws, he admitted. Actually, the flaws were far from minor. It would be spring of 1889 before the exhausted inventor was able to present an improved phonograph.

Soon Al was dreaming once again of new uses for his favorite invention. The phonograph could be used to "read" books to the blind, his dreams told him. Teachers could use it for giving instructions. Tiny phonographs could be used to make talking dolls, whistling toy engines, barking animals, and chirping birds. It could make clocks and watches call out the time of day. It most certainly could be used to record music. And wouldn't it be wonderful if the Statue of Liberty in New York Harbor could speak to the crowds entering their new land? The possibilities were endless. It was time to get back to work.

Afterword

The phonograph is just a small part of the story of Thomas Alva Edison. He and his workers were responsible for countless other inventions, from the electric light to the motion picture camera. "He invents all the while, even in his sleep," Mina Edison said.

Al and Mina were married for forty-five years. They had three children, Madeleine, Charles, and Theodore. Thomas Edison died at the age of eighty-four on October 18, 1931, in West Orange, New Jersey. During his lifetime, he patented more than one thousand inventions. The phonograph was his favorite.

Thomas Edison's
Major Inventions

Improved Telegraph
Mimeograph
Improved Telephone
Phonograph
Electric Light
Improved Electric Generator
Electric-powered Train
Improved Motion Picture Camera
Alkaline Storage Battery

This is not a complete list of Thomas Edison's inventions. During his lifetime, Edison was responsible for hundreds of inventions, including many improvements of other people's work.

Bibliography

Conot, Robert. *A Streak of Luck: The Life and Legend of Thomas Alva Edison.* New York: Seaview Books, 1979.

Dyer, Frank Lewis, and Thomas Commerford Martin. *Edison: His Life and Inventions.* New York: Harper & Brothers, 1929.

Jenkins, Reese V., ed. *The Papers of Thomas Edison.* Vol. 3, *The Making of an Inventor, February 1847-June 1873.* Baltimore: The Johns Hopkins University Press, 1989.

Josephson, Matthew. *Edison: A Biography.* New York: McGraw Hill Book Co., 1959.